ARE YOU HAPPY

MOMINUL AMIN

MOM and DAD

Contents

Foreword

We have tried our best to present this book in front of you. Hope the book will not disappoint you. If you find any part of the book to be incorrect, please let me know and I will do my best to correct it.

Preface

no word say

Acknowledgements

The chapters of this book are taken from the lives of different people. I thank each and every person very much. Because there are so many educated and intelligent people around us. That we can never imagine. From them we learn such and such chapters of life. Which may not be possible to learn by reading all the books of a famous author. I started writing this book by thanking all those people. Who teach people like us many big chapters of life. Totally free.

Prologue

Today, problems have surrounded us in such a way that it has become very difficult to survive even if we are well. We actually forgot what We need to be well. This book will help you stay well and make the right decisions in life. It will help you build good relationships with people around you.

Second Edition

Why is this the second edition of the book? Why was this book rewritten? There are many reasons behind it facing many problems.

This book was the first book of my life. That's why I had very little experience. Moreover, since I did not study literature, I Literary knowledge was negligible. As a result, there were many mistakes in this book, especially in spelling. And also the big problem was that this book was completely deleted from me. As a result, I was not able to access the book "Is it so hard to be good".

I had to rename the book "Is it so hard to be good" and rename the book to "Why are we not good"?

Everything in this book has been revised and written as much as possible. Hope there will be no more mistakes after that. Since we are humans, if there are any mistakes or errors, please let us know so that we can completely change it in the next version. And can give a proper useful book to the public. I hope you will show us enough love in this book as before.

Mominul Amin

Author Word

Why did I write the book? Why should you read the book? I will try to answer these questions. If I don't share some things with you, I might feel a little bad. So I am sharing the words with you. I want you to hear these words. First of all why the name of the book is what it is I have told the story beautifully below why I gave the name of the book this way. So first I have been thinking for several days to write a book. At first, I was thinking of writing about several topics. Ever thought to write a romantic story? But again I thought that I should write a romantic story. Then I thought maybe I will write a book about ethical hacking. I have also written about 10 pages. Then no more writing. I spend about four to five months writing and writing. Then one night I decided to write a new book. That will be useful for all of us. And from that, I wrote 'Is it very difficult to be good?' When I first started writing, I thought I would write 200 to 300 pages. But when I sat down to write, after writing 10 pages, I felt that I had written all the ideas in my head in 10 pages. Then I thought that this book might not be written like other books. Then I was very worried about it. Because I could not write and write and write for a long time. Then decide to stop all work and write the book first. And immediately decided that I had to take a break from all my phones, and social media for a while. And I switched off all my phones. Then for about 14 days, I was completely isolated from the people of the world. I was locked in a room. In between, I read more than a hundred books by different authors. I'm surprised to think I did it in just 14 days. Maybe if someone gave me 365 days, I would be so many

I could never finish reading the book. Maybe it's to be determined. The people who are most surprised to see me are my parents. He always saw me busy on the phone. But suddenly I was studying for 14 to 15 hours and it was the most amazing thing they had ever seen. I was surprised. What I understand from this is that if we do it, we may never be able to do it. But if we become determined and think we will do it. Then of course we will complete it. For the first time, I was always active day and night, meaning whenever I remembered any new information, I immediately noted it in the notebook. And at the end of the day, I wrote it down. In this way, I wrote about 150 pages. I mean, I'm amazed to think that 150 pages have gone through my head. Amazing.

I'm not saying you can change the world by reading this book. But what I will say is that if you read this book, you will change yourself a little bit. At least a little will change your way of thinking. Many of the things written in the book have been written down by my feelings. And I am not an experienced writer. I have never studied literature, so I don't know much about literature, because I am a science student. So if there are any mistakes in the writing, please let me know on my social media and I will try to correct them. And I will make sure that such mistakes do not happen again. This is my first book so I have no experience in that way. My intention is not to earn money by selling books. So if you want you can download and read this book in any way. I will be happy if you read it. Because I intend that you should read this book if at all in your life

I will feel very fortunate if you can make a difference. That I could come to your service. I have no bad intentions behind writing this book. Why I felt that maybe you need to read a book like this. Maybe if you read this book you will learn to be good. Start giving yourself time.

We always try to change the people around us but if you read the book you might start changing yourself first. Because I can change the people around me and the world only if I change myself first.

I may indeed have completed this book in 14 days but I have 18 years of experience in writing this book. I tried to write this book by learning from my own experiences. I don't know how you will like the book, but I hope so

will need

I tried to talk about the little things of our life, I don't know how much I managed to convey to you. But I tried my best.

We have tried to explain to you little by little about everything from our studies to love so that we can find the right purpose in our life.

Because life is ours, we have to fulfill our purpose. Otherwise, if we give it to others, they can play with our life. Much in the same way that when we give our favorite things to others, it is not a love to them but a need for them. We need to understand these things.

In doing so I finished the book. I would like to write more books if you wish. I will write them down.

You will be fine and take care of yourself.

Mominul Amin

MOMINUL AMIN

PROFILE

Book writter, motivational speaker, ethical hacker, you tuber,app creater, website developer etc
Date of birth=12/12/2001

Our another book

Contact us

Facebook= @mominul_amin
The MOMI
@iwayofhaven
Instagram=@mominul_amin
@the__momi
@momi_universe
Twitter=@the___momi
@mominul_amin
Email=workwiththemomi@gmail.com

Mominul Amin

"LIFE IS A GIFT GIVEN
BY GOD, WHICH WE HAVE
NO RIGHT TO WASTE"

Mominul Amin

ONE

ARE YOU GOOD?

Hello, are you good?

Did you have a good day?

The people you spend every day with, do they care about you?

At the end of the day, do they ask you how your day was?

Ever get upset at the end of the day?

Ever wanted to die?

Do you ever feel that if you had done that in the past, maybe you would be a little better than the situation you are in today? Sleep well at night. This time, you are not angry with me?

The people of the world do not think that they are playing with you.

Don't get angry with your parents, and don't feel like they're trying to fulfill their dreams through you that they couldn't.

And these dreams of theirs seem understandable to you.

Never thought it would change the world.

Never thought that tomorrow would be better.

You never wanted to buy something that you want, but maybe you can't afford it.

Are you finally happy?

I mean are you good?

If any of the above questions have happened to you or are similar to one of them,

Then the book is for you or my words are for you.

Are we asking too much of society?

Not at all?

I just want to be a little happy, a little better.

Is that what we get?

I don't have to answer the above questions, do the questions yourself and answer yourself.

See the answers you are giving yourself, are you giving them from your heart, are you satisfied with the answers you are giving in vain?

hope not

There is no word

The one I want wants someone else

The first thing is, do I know or do we know why we want him?

Or?

We want to do something big in life. Or we want to be a businessman or a great photographer. So maybe we don't mind our studies at all. So maybe our reading seems like a burden.

So what?

So what do we want to do in life, have we done some of it, better said?

I mean, the things we want to do in life, do you think you want to be a photographer?

But have you clicked any good photos till now, which is enough for you to become a photographer?

Didn't, that's why. That means you want to be a photographer but don't want to work hard on it.

Isn't that so?

Another thing we always say or we always complain about is that no one in the world understands us, parents, brothers, sisters, and even friends.
Do you understand yourself?
I don't think so.
so
I did not want to confuse you by asking so many questions.
My only intention was that through my words you can recognize yourself even a little.
Because if we don't know ourselves.
Then the people of the world will know us.
not so
Do you love someone?
If yes, then he must have hurt you sometimes or hurt you with his words or behavior.
Maybe you wanted to explain the words to him, but you were afraid.
If I say that I am hurt because of your reasons, then maybe I will quarrel with you.
The biggest one, he can leave.
This is not scary.
And if you are not in love with someone or simple words you are single.
For you to be single in your friend circle, your friends may have questioned your worthiness to marry a girl.
Isn't that so?
Your friend's expensive car looks like an expensive phone
Do you also want to buy it?
May not be able to buy due to poor financial conditions.
So maybe you are proud of God.
Maybe you are more qualified to carry an expensive phone or an expensive car than your friend who walks around with an expensive car, or an expensive phone.

so

Have you ever thought that your friends may have gotten good results because they attended a good college or school? Maybe because you didn't get the benefits

Your results are not as high as you expected.

Isn't it boring?

Oh no no I'm not boring you guys.

I am just raising the questions in your mind for once.

Because it is best to ask yourself.

Oh, I forgot.

How do you ask yourself?

Because you don't have time. After spending most of the day on the phone, maybe you couldn't find time for yourself.

You don't question yourself like that.

That's why you have to give yourself some time.

You can wait all day for the girl you love.

But see you couldn't make time for yourself.

Then how will the people of the world talk to you by repeating their times?

Do you think that the situation you have now will last for the rest of your life?

I mean if you are fine.

Or pass the day by having fun with friends. And think that in this way the whole life may pass or you can pass it.

And if you're bad, do you think you'll be bad for the rest of your life?

No boss you won't stay.

Remember that everything in the world has its opposite.

And if you are well, be prepared for the danger ahead.

And if you are bad.

But give good news to your mind,

That your good times are coming.

Do you believe in God?

If you are doing it is good. If you are not doing it, then start doing it.
Whether God exists or not will at least give you peace of mind.
Because even for a while, you will throw your problems on God's shoulders.
Hey, that's what's needed.
You cannot carry all the burdens of the world alone.
Hey you man
From burdening yourself with all your pains, you don't realize that you leave something to someone, thinking of them as God.
If you ask me personally,
Who do you believe in God?
But the answer would be yes.
But I am a very God-fearing person.
Hey, I always feel like God is watching me.
As a result of which the question arises in the mind even before doing any bad work,
What should be done?
As a result, I can't do that.
But God did not forbid me.
But because I fear God
It was not done by me.
Here is the profit money.
my
Only by believing in God.
I didn't have to think too much about this.
Don't think at all.
are you well Instead of wanting to hear this from others, ask yourself once every day, Am I really good?
If the answer is no, you need to do whatever it takes to improve. You need yourself most to take care of yourself.

TWO

Is it too hard to be good?

I don't think so.
We may not know exactly.
That is exactly how happy or how well we should be.
I became sad for no reason.
Don't assume that while walking on the street or while chatting in a shop, a stranger comes and makes a bad comment on our name, we get upset.
But whose words we are upset. No, he knows me. No, I know him.
Then hold again.
Suppose you went to play in the field in the afternoon.
You may have gone to play for,
If you go to the field, your body will also be good. A little light body will take the air.
He went to the field and saw some boys playing cricket.
You also started playing cricket with them.
Maybe you got out on the first ball.
Just look and your mind will say,
Nothing will happen to me.

No, you intended to go to the field!
Playing cricket is the purpose of your life, so what was the need to say that?
Where did you go to the field to freshen yourself up? But he returned home with disappointment.
Do we need all these thoughts?
What did we read all day today?
What did I do?
what game
But you see, more than that we care that,
What did a village boy do today?
Which boy got a job?
Who is the new girlfriend?
Who bought a new smartphone?
Who buys a new bike?
Who bought the new house?
These things are of little interest to us, aren't they?
Is it necessary at all?
Because we don't have the above things or what we have may not be of that quality.
We suffer, and we feel sorry for ourselves.
You know those you are suffering for.
You hate talking about money.
They are damn good.
We can determine a lot of our life if we want. Likewise, our well-being is also completely in our hands.
Let me tell you a little story.
I like to be a little nicer. I don't know why, I want everything to be perfect. Everything from clothing. So that day I was going to meet a friend of mine. Me and my friend named Devjit. I didn't know how to ride a bike so when I go out I take someone with me. On the way, suddenly it starts raining. So we have to stop at one place before reaching

Granthabba place. At that place, there was a veranda in front of the house. And we entered that balcony, myself Devjit and another old man on a bicycle. So there was a sack and I sat on that sack. And in front of me stood my friend Devjit and the old man the same bicycle he had come on was doing What happens if it rains and rains?

So I asked Devjit to bring tea and he went to bring tea. It was just me and the old man on the balcony. Suddenly my eyes went to the man's pocket and I saw there a note for 100 rupees and two ten rupees. And that's when I noticed my shoes. Looking at his feet, he felt very small. Who am I showing so much pride? Or who am I showing these to?

A man's whole day's worth of earnings I read as shoes.

I don't know why, that day I and the old man seemed to be side by side, but despite that, it seemed that I, the older man, came from two completely different worlds. I have many needs and dreams. And the old man's only demand is to go home when the rain stops.

Looking into his eyes and face, I saw no pain, no sorrow.

For a while everything I had seemed insignificant to him. I don't know why that day the man seemed to be much richer than us. He is much better than us.

He doesn't want to prove anything to anyone. He wants to present it to people just like that. People can think about what they want about him. I looked down and saw that everything I had was perfect. And nothing about that man was perfect. But he thinks he is the best in himself.

And that day I got the real formula of being well.

We don't need all we are looking for to have a little smile to be well.

There is no end to our needs. Our needs are endless.

There are so many problems in our life.

I don't know exactly how much money we need to live well.

Because when we start earning we forget everything and just start earning. Then one day we die.
I am not saying that we don't need money to survive.
Of course, there is a lot needed.
But we have to stop sometime, don't we?
You must try to move forward but I will never forget what you have.
We suffer ourselves to keep our loved ones well. Sometimes I struggle to keep my family well.
You know your family members can never be good if you are suffering.
And those who are fine with hurting you are at least not your family members.
So understand things a little.

THREE
LIFE IS A TEST

You see, we have all heard one thing. That is.
Adapt to the situation
If not, change the situation.‘
It means that if your condition is bad, be it financially or physically, start adapting to it, or if it is very difficult for you to adapt or accept, then try to change it.
Otherwise, you will never be happy in life.
What is most interesting is that,
We always do something for this in life. So that after doing this we don't have to work anymore. For example, not everyone knows that business is more money than government jobs, but why everyone rushes after government jobs because they think that if they get the job once, then they may not have to work anymore. It means we are very lazy. We always want to be good. Being good again for us means sitting quietly without working. The best is if someone tells us that we sit quietly at home and I will pay you month by month then this is the best life for us.
Let me explain it to you simply. In my reading room, there is a piece of paper pasted in a place "Never try to change what you cannot change but try to adapt to it. Because there are

many things that you can never change no matter how hard you try. Those things are most beneficial to us or our well-being if we start accepting them.

We must understand that life is a test. This test will continue as long as we live. If you think that maybe you are being tested now and if you do the work you are doing then maybe you will never have another test in your life. causes Because whenever you reach that point, you are not ready for the rest of the tests, which is why you will fail miserably in life.

You will see when we were in school when we heard about the exam, we used to get scared. The exam was like going to that operational theater for us. But if you remember on the other side, you will see that many who were in the first stage of the class were very happy to hear about this exam. We study in the same class as you, we can be said to be of the same age. So why ws a source of fear for us and a source of joy for them.?The reason is only that that they know that one day the exam will come and that's why they start preparing for the exam little by little from the very first day. So when the exam day comes they are happy because they have prepared themselves completely for that exam. On the other hand, boys like us were not prepared for that exam, so it was a source of fear and and sadness for us.

Do you know what is the most interesting thing when the first-class students hear about the exam, they imagine good results, parents' joy, and teachers' and children's cheers.

And when we used to hear about exams, bad results, scolding from parents, humiliation from teachers, etc. came to our head.

Life is like that you just need to understand that you will be tested at every stage of life. Sometimes the exams will be very difficult for you which you will not be able to solve easily, and some exams will be passed in a very short time. As with school students sometimes very difficult questions and sometimes very easy questions.

But the most important thing is that you have to attend these exams. Otherwise, this life will have zero meaning. If you think about it if there were no tests in the world, how would we judge who is competent in studies or academically? How we hire a good teacher for our boys. But we can go from one step to another because the tests are there. Just because there are these tests in life, I can improve myself from one stage to another.

I hope that from today onwards, whenever you fall into a bad situation, you will think with a light smile that this small test, I was already prepared for it.

FOUR

LIFE IS UNFAIR

I have written a lot on many topics. But it was the biggest test for me whenever I thought of starting to write about Life is Fair. It is a phase of our life that may or may not have come into the life of every human being. Because believe it or not doing what you want to do in life is indeed going to be very difficult for you at some point, I mean pretty much like this. You may not get what you want out of life, you may get more or less. can

What does life is unfair to mean? Let me first explain to you why life is not equal for everyone. The amount of work you are doing to achieve a task or your goal in life and even after working so hard you are not reaching the right people. This is fine so far but you will have trouble only when you see that A friend of yours has achieved the goal you want to achieve with even less effort.

Again you may be fulfilling your desires little by little in life suppose you bought a bike after some time and then after a few years you bought a four-wheeler. It's nice to think about it on the one hand but the bad thing is when you've been working hard to get these things and one of your friends is walking around with them, you'll feel like you've worked so hard to own that thing and there are a lot of people. Who is enjoying the life of their dreams without any effort? Finances come then life is not equal for everyone. Life is unfair because then you keep blaming your luck why this is happening to me? Or have I done so much wrong that I have to get the punishment? So why has God made the paths so difficult for me? Because we didn't want much from God, we wanted to keep ourselves well, we wanted to fulfill our dreams.

I am working hard enough for that, so why am I not getting those things? Why do people around me work less hard to get them?

Why do bad things only happen to me?

Have you ever thought about it?

Hope the course came?

Such thoughts have occurred to me many times. Because I am human too and I am a thinking person like you.

For example, let's tell a story

A few days ago, a friend of mine told me that every day, you know, that friend of mine travels around with his bike and many friends all the time. They are enjoying life. We still cannot enjoy life. I didn't say anything to him just kept quiet. After some time I got a call from my friend who was riding his bike. I called him and asked him what happened. On the other side, he said I am in great danger. Did I ask why? He replied that the friends I was drinking with made a video of me and humiliated me in front of my family. And I didn't understand when they secretly made a video of me and now they are showing different people that I drink. Then a few days passed before the friend told me or the friend who regretted telling me one day how bad his friends were.

I told him a few days ago that you wanted such friends. So

why are you feeling bad now? What is the biggest problem? The internet world has been revolutionized in such a way. We are always surrounded by such people who are established today. And we feel that some of them have become successful overnight. We always see their successful life. Seeing their wrong life makes us feel like we should have had the life.

Trust me, you can't imagine how many pillow-wet nights these people have had to get the success you see or the mountain of hard work they put in.

If I ask you to do his work, you will not want to do it.

So if I simply say that life is fair is completely wrong. It is only a vision. Which we only consider from one side. Because things that seem unfair to you are like dreams to other people and things that are unfair to other people are like dreams to you. Our biggest problem is that we always want to enjoy the next life and not our own.

This is why we can never be good.

We are always greedy for the next life.

Things that seem unfair to you or things that seem to have happened to you badly.

Think about them again and again and think about why you call them bad thoughts.

Like, let me tell you a little thing. For example, since I was a child, I was alone most of the time because I studied in a hostel. When I came home, I didn't interact with anyone like that. My friend said only Rabindranath Sambari, Bankim Sambar, and also Arabic Rajini novels. I used to read only these in my spare time. There were so many complaints about your life, I always thought that God was not good to me. Because I have no friends, etc.

Then slowly when I grew up and started mixing with people, I found that I knew many things that other boys of my age did not know. Because I read a lot of books during the times when I was alone. And these were my advantages. Maybe that's why I wrote the book today. So at that time, that thing was unfair to me but now it is an advantage for me in that thing. Life is like that, what we have to do is to use the bad things in our life as advantages. Indeed, at that time you will not feel that it will benefit you. But believe me, slowly you will get the answer, and one day you will feel that everything that happens to you has only benefited you. Be it someone leaving or someone dying.

What you need to do in between is to move forward from the good. And the more you worry about the people around you, the more you will suffer, so don't worry about the people around you, but think about yourself when you have time. So I say, again and again, think about the bad things that happened to you, you will find the answer. That's how far you have to go. no Making it easier for you to be where you are today. Think about it because bad things happened to you in the past but you are in this situation today. Maybe you are not good at what you wanted but in some other way, you have improved yourself more than before. So give yourself plenty of time. Find yourself before you find the world You are an invaluable resource. Discover yourself a little bit every day. When you discover yourself a little bit every day you will be surprised and you will start to think that you have so much in me. But don't be arrogant. It is the greatest gift given to us by God or Allah.

FIVE

ONE MISTAKE IS ENOUGH

Just as we eat food every day, we make mistakes every day. Making mistakes is not a crime. It is just as well to make a mistake but it is also a big crime. The most important thing is that no matter how hard we try?
We cannot completely avoid doing the wrong thing or doing wrong from our life. All we can do is gradually reduce this error. I mean if I put it simply then the thing stands like this. If you were wrong in 100 days before, maybe after reading my words or this book it will be 15 or 10. And if someone tells you that he will prevent you from making a complete mistake.
Then believe that he is completely lying to you or he must have some ulterior motive behind it.
The funniest thing is to make mistakes but nothing bad at all. Rather, through this mistake or because we constantly make mistakes, but we are improving ourselves little by little every day. You remember when you used to write 'A' on the blackboard and erase it repeatedly with a piece of cloth or to put it simply because you made mistakes again and

again and erased it with a piece of cloth but today you have learned to speak Bengali completely or learn the rest of the letters completely.

Or because you fell repeatedly when you were young but you learned to walk. Because of these small mistakes, you are in the right place today.

So to put it more simply, the more mistakes we make, the more we can improve. But the biggest problem is that we have to determine exactly how much wrong is right for us and how much wrong can harm us or will be accepted as wrong for us.

I will try to explain to you in this chapter what is wrong and what is right for you.

If I put it more simply, I will give you an idea so that when you do something wrong, you can at least think about how harmful or beneficial it is for you.

I would like to share with you several facts. Through the events you can guess which mistakes are good for you and which mistakes are bad for you.

Incident-1

I had an illegitimate brother. He was an employee of a shop, so he suddenly came home at twelve noon one day, he came home and asked his mother what is there from the kitchen today, his mother told him the answer.

There are potatoes, rice, poppy seeds and pulses.

He got very angry and he angrily said that every day the same kind of curry, I will not eat anymore. As she screamed profusely, her father ran from the next room and slapped her on the cheek.

He had a shirt around his neck and he immediately left the house by turning towards his room. It was evening but he still did not return home when his family started looking for him. After a lot of searching, I suddenly got information that he had gone to the side of the railway line. There was a railway line near his village then everyone went towards the railway line. I went there and saw that his head and lower body were completely separated. Different parts of his body were spread over the line.

The incident that I heard above, you will see this kind of incident happening with you or around you. We make such mistakes but what we don't do is we don't choose suicide like that boy. But the rest of the anger thing we do but my reason behind telling this story is that if we continue to do such things then we should be careful in advance that one day our consequences may be such terrible. Because most of the mistakes we make are intentional. And when we are angry, our head does not work.

Event-2

I had a friend named Rehan. The friend was quite talented, moreover, he was from a quite high-class family. Even the boy's view of the world was visually different. Bro you are not easily fooled. And he loved himself most of all. And that's why he didn't have a girlfriend. He had a friend. Ryan knew that he didn't need a lot of people to survive or be well. So he only hung out with that friend and did everything. In fact, that friend always took small help from Ryan.

Most of the time they used to hang out together. As a result, his relationship with the rest of his friends was almost severed. And slowly he did not realize when he became dependent on his friend. Means whenever he had to go somewhere he depended on one person and that was the friend.

This was when his friend realized this.

Used him a lot.

She would tell her stories as she wished, whenever she felt

like calling her. But when Rehan used to call, he would not receive the call. If asked why you are not answering my calls, he would say I was busy.

Similarly if Rehan ever misses a call. Then he was very angry with her.

And this thing was hurting Rehan from inside.

Every time Rehan tried to tell her that these things made her feel bad. Then that friend would look at him angrily and say that it is ok then no need to call from today. Rihan immediately apologized to him.

This made Rehan break from inside. If Rehan ever went somewhere with someone then that boy would be very angry why he didn't tell him. That means he doesn't care about him. But his friend would do everything when he wanted to talk to other people.

Every day Rehan was suffering a little bit because of this. But because he didn't want to break the relationship, he tolerated everything. Rehan has been in the relationship for so long and what is the need to break it.

Sometimes he would always ask his friend to spend 200 rupees while traveling. When Ryan spent 400 500 rupees behind him, he did not consider them as money. To do this, Rehan used to borrow money from different people and give him money every day. Rehan's amount of money or loan amount became so much that one day he committed suicide.

The incident that I told you, you will see this kind of incident with your girlfriend or friend, maybe you have seen it in front of your eyes.

No matter how smart we are, sometimes we make big mistakes without realizing it. Ryan was quite educated and even intelligent.

But it proved a great folly by committing suicide.

We often become dependent on many people without realizing it. People who enter our lives like a virus. If you don't see a doctor, if you don't recognize the people at the right time, then you will continue to make mistakes and when that mistake will take a big shape or like a virus that will destroy your life. enough to cause or disturb your well-being.

Whenever you find yourself getting addicted to something it can be anything. Try to fix it early before you make a big mistake. Be it a female friend or pornography.

These small mistakes do not allow us to be good. These flowers are slowly killing us. No matter how wise you are, when these mistakes happen to you, or when such things happen to you, you become emotional. So there's no need to ever sacrifice or show extra love to anyone except your own family. As many times as you sacrifice yourself for those people, they won't leave you until you're completely gone. Such a wrong relationship or a wrong person will kill you. It's not just that you won't be well. Each of your tasks will be disrupted equally. And you will continue to hurt those people who treat you well without knowing it. Therefore, try to restrain yourself completely from mistakes.

Now I will talk about some mistakes that are very necessary in our life. Those mistakes are like when you think you failed an exam or you were doing a task with too much effort and you failed, mistakes will teach you to do that task better and make you a fully experienced person. And it will tell you about your abilities. Sir when you know what kind of work or in what manner you can do. Then it will make you happy. As a result, your life will be very easy and it will be very easy for you to be well.

SIX

FRIEND FRIEND FRIEND

friend friend friend
The companion of our happiness is the companion of our sorrow
Even our partners in bad deeds.
How we live depends a lot on the people around us.
You know that.
It means that what we will do and how we will live is largely in the hands of our friends.
It's a bit surprising but it's true.
You might be thinking that all these things are in our own hands.
Then you are thinking wrong.
For example, suppose you have four friends with whom you spend most of your free time. Each of them has little to say except for you. They spend most of the day intoxicated or playing games.
If you say something good to them.
Say something about the purpose of life, then they will ignore you.

You will remember once you stay.
Let's play games with them.
This way you will never realize that your game has become addictive by playing games with them.
Or maybe you've become a full-fledged drug addict yourself after a cigarette or two from them.
You won't understand.
Again suppose you have five friends. Each of them has a purpose in life. You have no purpose in life. And only you eat cigarettes in your group.
Then you will see that when you listen to the conversation of your friends, you also have a purpose in life. Just like they don't smoke cigarettes. So you also can't smoke cigarettes while with them.
So slowly you too will come out of addiction.
Now you understand.
What we become or what we think depends a lot on the people we are with.
I'm not judging anyone here.
I am just trying to make you understand the reality. No, I don't like smoking cigarettes, or cigarettes.
Try to understand the language of what I said.
Now again we prefer real people or afternoon chats with friends.
Give more time to Facebook friends.
not so
We always say. Who is how many friends? Today he uploaded the picture. How many likes did it get? Who reacted? We like to think more of these. Some time ago, a study revealed that a person can only speak 10% of what he can talk to virtual people.
Or suppose your mother fell ill yesterday. Will your Facebook friends come?

Of course, the answer will be no.

When you know they won't come. So is it worth spending so much time on them?

Of course not, isn't it?

Again our friend will be angry because he gets admission to this school or college. To make him happy we also admitted.

Whatever our goal in life is.

We make friends now and then.

We think we are making friends.

After some time, I see that those friends are the ones who trouble us.

There are many reasons why we are bad.

I'm not forbidding you to be friends, just trying to understand who you're going to be friends with.

I'm not asking to match her lineage. All I'm saying is that before friending or trusting someone, check if the person you're going to friend is a good fit for you.

If the answer is yes, then definitely make it.

But if not, never go for it.

You might be thinking hey just making a friend. If you think so much, you will not be able to mix with anyone.

That's why I asked you first if you want to be well.

I want to be happy in my life.

And for that, you have to accept or start accepting everything little by little.

You are the category of people who want to be well.

You may feel that you have asked for little. But you know what you are looking for the most valuable thing in the world is to be well.

We like to be alone most of the time.

It is good to say that as the present age progresses, we are slowly becoming lonely.

If you notice, you will see that you don't hang out with your friends like you used to, you don't go out with your friends like you used to, you don't even go to the cinema and watch the movie, that is, the places where you can meet people more. You may not like all the places you used to go to. He likes to spend more time with his phone at home. Now let me tell you frankly. Just as some friends are bad for us, a good friend is enough for us. I don't think you need to make more than one friend. It is enough if you make a good friend in the right way.

Now you might say that it is very difficult to find good friends these days.

Are you good friends or not?

Absolutely.

Not believing?

If you think I am friends with you then are you, my bad friend?

Are you bad yourself, as a friend?

Or,

So?

You see one thing we always hear is that no friend is good.

Everyone just needs to mix.

Then you are thinking wrong.

Think for yourself, don't think lightly but think deeply.

The friends you make yourself.

Do you just mix with them? If you think very deeply, you will see that there is no name.

You will also see some hidden interests. Maybe your interest is smaller than the person in front. But there are interests.

If you are selfless. So what will the rest do?

Let me make it clear

At first, you think you have just a few very good friends. Who will rush to you in times of danger? Don't forget your friends. But think only of that friend who always rushes to your word. At the same time think that he comes to you without any interest of his own.

If you have one name in your Uttara then you are a very lucky person. And if the answer is no, then this is for you. or me for you If you don't have such a good friend till now, I will tell you why.

Have you ever been in danger of them?

Have you ever listened to their words?

Have they stood by their side when they were in danger?

Have they asked how they are at the end of the day?

were you happy now When you had a good time? Have you ever remembered them?

Have you ever made them share your happiness?

Think carefully. Answer: It will not come.

When you think about what you have done, you feel like you did it all with your mind.

Of course, you did it on purpose.

But you could not make them their people.

The first thing is that relationships should always be selfless. Meaning if you associate with someone selflessly. Then you will see with whom you mix selflessly. He may not be treating you the way you treat him. But if you think about it a little more, you will see that someone is taking care of you selflessly with you. Even listening to you.

A little smile is coming, right?

Yes, that's the real trick, we don't recognize the people who love us but we can't forget the people who dislike us. Just think of them and feel like there is no one by our side.

Just as some people dislike you, many people love you selflessly.

So give love to those who love instead of those who hurt you and you will find good real friends.

We don't need a lot of friends to have good faith.
One friend is enough
That does not mean that I forbid you to socialize with other friends. For example, if you study in college, about your college friends, if you work in an office, then about your office colleagues, if you go to play in the afternoon, then I am talking about the friendship of your players.
Associate with them but never involve yourself with them.
Unless one of them is your true friend.
Socialize with them first.
Give it some time.
Whom you make him close to you. They will hurt you too.
First, treat a friend as you would expect to be treated. You don't have to do anything else and he will give you the best treatment you deserve.
Yes, but it will take some time.
It means you made friends with a stranger. And the treatment you show him is your best treatment. So at first you might sit hoping that he will treat you very well.
Then you are wrong.
He'll start ignoring you after you've been gone for a while.
Ignore him.
Because you know that you have done everything selflessly with him. Then rest assured. He will remember you just when someone leaves him with the same disdain.
This is real.
Tell us what our main problem is the things that bad people stay with us. When they are with us we see their bad qualities but only when they leave me.
Surprisingly, it is true that we remember their very good qualities.
And their bad qualities seem insignificant to us.
We are just such a nation.

Do you understand?

Once you become a good friend of someone, you will be surprised to see that you will never lack a good friend.

By now you must have understood how much we need friends. When I say friend here, I mean good friend. You must understand by now how you should behave. Now I will tell you who you want to live with as friends. How to find them or know if they deserve to be your true friend?

Told you first to pick a good friend first. You start it. First, we will make good friends with those who are already in our life. Let me also help you make good friends.

The first thing to look for when choosing a friend or someone in your life is Just how much he respects not just you but other people.

What you will notice most is how much he respects people who are poorer than him. or how to treat them. It is important to see that maybe he respects you but not others. Then remember that the respect he gives you is not genuine at all. There must be a big reason why he has given you respect today. He is giving you that respect to get something from you. So be sure that the day you stop giving him that thing he will stop respecting you. So if such friends are already in your life then get away from them as soon as you can. And who speaks with great respect not only to you but to every person who is with him. Relatives associate. Then make him a good friend in your life. And rest assured that if you are ever in danger or if your condition ever deteriorates, he will always be by your side. And if you don't have such people in your life then you keep looking for such people. If you get them make friends and stay happy.

The second thing that you will do or the quality that you will look for in your friend is that the friend does not give much importance to what people around him call him.

They like to stay very simple. He is happy just as God made him. Then you remember that no matter what you are, he will always be by your side.

Thirdly, the most important thing to notice is how much money you spend while traveling. I mean if you ever go out with him you will see him telling you to buy this and buy that. That makes you spend a huge amount every time you go out with them. So stay away from all those friends. Because they have come to destroy you.

Watch out in the same way if a friend forbids you from spending. Or if he pays the bill at a restaurant, remember that you are very lucky. A good friend has been found. make him

Fourth, see if the person you have made a friend or want to make is lying or not.

If the answer is yes.

Then slowly move away. You may have a question in your mind that everyone lies these days. No, I didn't tell that kind of lie to tell lie.

Who lies to other friends in front of you who lie about important things? Remember that he will lie about you in front of other friends.

So stay away from such friends.

Fifth, this is one of the most important things you will see in your friends.

Exactly how much they value you. It means that you will see many friends who need you in their needs or if they need any of their work. Then he talks to you so sweetly, as if there is no one better than you in his life.

But when you need them, they don't answer your phone properly. Even months go by without calling you.

Then you can be sure that you will never find them in your danger.

They only associate with you when they need to. Nothing more than that. So they are very dangerous. They can tell you anything when they need you. You can do a lot of names. So always try to stay away from them.
They are the real selfish ones
They have never loved anyone but themselves.
So if you have such friends, remove them from your friend list now.

The sixth thing is that you will see that everyone has a goal in our life. Meaning life purpose is what you want to do in life. Or what things you want to work on when you grow up. Whenever you say all those things in front of your friends, they just laugh at you or say that you can't do these things. Why are you doing these things?
Do the things we do. A lot of money to our wwork Keep in mind that people who don't respect your way of thinking can never be your friends. Or can't be your happy partner. So your valuable comments will not be useful in the way of life with them.
I don't want him to listen to you.
So never tell such friends about your dreams.
The seventh thing to emphasize is to stay away from friends who are crazy about getting attention from people. It means that you are in a circle of friends. There is a friend who is discussing something and everyone is listening to it. All of a sudden your friend comes and starts talking about himself. Every friend in that circle started to feel annoyed. And you expect them to listen to you. They are so crazy about getting attention from people that your name is in front of you and other people's names inare front of others. Remember that in the same way that discrediting others in front of you confirms your disrepute in front of others. Because they always want to be good to everyone. And this

is why everyone talks about everyone.

So never share important things or secrets of your life with them. He will always share your secret with everyone, so if you want to live, stay away from these friends today.

The eighth thing that is very interesting is how he treats his family membersNoticece that. It means he doesn't listen to his family. Notice if his parents oppose it. Remember that what cannot be your family can be yours. So you must pay attention to this thing.

You will see that he values his family more or less than you. If you see that someone from his family may have given him one but he is not picking up the phone because he is with you then don't think that he is giving you more importance. Rather think abothan ut it, he doesn't care about his family. He only cares about what he needs so always try triesstay away from such friends.

How is he to the people of the ninth society. ?f you see that everyone speaks against him. That means, remember that there must be some error in it. If that person is very close to you, find out his fault and tell him.

You are very lucky if he listens to you and corrects the mistake, but if he doesn't, you will think he is only thinking about himself. So hanging out with him means making yourself worse in the eyes of society. So you are unknowingly making yourself unemployable to thciety. The less efeweres you make to keep yourself good, the better. So try to stay away from such friends.

Finally, the thing to focus on is the people you hang out with or consider to be good friends. What does your mind say to win your best friend?

Because if good friends don't feel you can never be happy with them. Can't be better to say more. So keep yourself away from them.

I did not mean to belittle anyone by what I said above. Just trying to explain what exactly you should do to keep yourself well. How to choose the right friends for your life. Because it depends on you how you will be good or bad.
If you want to keep yourself a little happy, you must live with good and honest friends.

SEVEN

THINKING ABOUT CAREER

"Dreams are not what we dream of
A dream is what keeps us awake."
If you remember the line, who would you say it to? The President of our country is APJ Abdul Kalam.
There are very few of us who have not heard the saying. But there are few people who know the true meaning of the saying.
Actually we all love to dream. Be it asleep or awake.
The dreams we see are beyond our control.
I'm not ruling out dreaming out of control, but we think that the dreams we're seeing may just be me. No one else sees.
So I am different from everyone, I am special.
I dream means I have a purpose in life. I think more than others.
If you think these things then you are thinking completely wrong. If you don't believe it, you go to the shop and have tea. Go ask him sometime. Ask about his dreams or ask your friends about their dreams. You will see that they dream

bigger than you. So dreaming is not a big deal. You know why I said this, because we all dream.

Dreaming is not a big deal. How hard are we working to make the dream a reality? Not just hard but how well we are doing it will determine whether my dreams will succeed.

You might be thinking, what does dreams have to do with being well?

Of course there is.

If we want to be well, we have to give great importance to everything. The most important thing is our thoughts and our dreams.

We dream but we don't know what we have to do to make the dream come true. Again many know but waiting to start.

If you don't believe me, I will tell you a story.

I have several YouTube channels like Daaran (The MOMI, The smart guide, cinematic expose, MOMI extraetc) whenever someone watches my channel videos especially my friends. They each said that they would also open YouTube channels themselves. They asked me how to open how to do what. I have told them to do this. Many of them tell me that they are willing to work with me. So what I do is give everyone some elements to make a video and tell them to make a video. Don't believe that maybe they all asked me one day to do as much as I have given them. So as usual I call after a day and ask if the job is done. It means the video has been made. Surprisingly everyone told me no. Some of them said that I really don't feel like doing the job. If you have other work, give it. And some people said hey, I only have one phone, that's why I couldn't make the video. And some people said give me some more time and I will make it. The ones I gave time to were not able to make the video till today whenever I call them they all say give me some more time.

Surprisingly, one of them made the video. He did not have any expensive phone. No, that boy was more educated. No he had multiple phones. But he made the video in the time it took me. What I wanted to convey to you through the above little incident is this. We don't really want to work. If you really wanted to work, you wouldn't just sit quietly and make excuses. But if you look outside and see what you want to do. You're not doing it for the same reason that someone else is doing it even though they have a bigger excuse. Honestly, if we want to do something, nothing can ever stop us. A reason is enough to do something. Just the same, enough of an excuse to do nothing. Whatever he wants to do, he will do it despite a thousand obstacles.

And those who really don't want to do it, no matter what you give them, they will find some excuse not to do it.

So if you want to do something in life then start it now.

If you think you can't do that, you're wrong.

Remember that if you can't do something, you can never do anything. Whatever you are doing, do it with your mind. You will see that your success is guaranteed.

Do you know what is one of our biggest faults?

We just don't like what we do when we do it. We like other things more and when we do other things we don't like those things but we like the work we were doing before.

Like when we go to any school we get wrong about every thing in school. For example, the school teachers are not good, they don't know how to teach, the school never has any program properly. Again, yes, the school next to us is better. The teachers of Rahul's school are better. But the sad thing is that when we get admission in Rahul's school, we discuss the bad things about that school and say hey there is nothing in the school. Everything was more convenient in the school I attended before.

Now understand our problem right here.

We ourselves do not know what we want. And that is why we are not good.

I will say one more thing. You will see that there is a very popular thing these days. Especially we hear through movies or social media that find your passion or find your talent then your life will be very easy.

And then we get confused. We wonder what talent we have. And what we see is that we have no talent. We can sing properly. No we look very nice. No, our father or mother has a lot of money and I will do whatever I want. Then we see a bit of disappointment. Then we remember that friend of mine sings well, that friend looks very good, etc.

Which lead us to depression. For no reason we continue to blaspheme God. God did not count anything in us so why sent him to earth only to be insulted to people.

He saw how bad our thinking is.

First of all, there is no such thing as talent. And if anyone thinks that there is such a thing as talent, then remember that there is definitely some talent in each of us. God didn't just make us. There must be some purpose behind its creation. He has created every thing in the world for some purpose. He never created anything without purpose.

Why do you think things like this for those who do not obey God?

Everyone thinks that we are a white paper that God has sent to some people with some talents means that he has written something on his white paper. And if you think that I have no talent, then you think that you have not written anything on your white paper. Then see how many benefits you have. You can write whatever you want on that white page according to your wish and even write as much as you want. And he who has something already written on his page does not have the right to do much in life. He has limited intelligence. But you have many options to prove yourself the best to the world.

Now you tell me who is really lucky?
Believe what you don't have rather than worrying about what you don't have. Again think about what you have. Honestly, if you count, you'll be happier than I am. You will find that you have so many things that you never thought possible before. The biggest thing is that the things you have may not be very good people. The thing that you have been thinking about for so long must have gone away.
Now let's see what we have to do. To say what we will do in life as a livelihood. Or which way to go. I think that is the first thing you need before asking this question. First you need to know things well and know them from good people. Because every decision we make depends on our past thoughts. Better to say it depends on past experience.
If we don't choose the right way to earn a living then we can never live well.
So to stay well we have to look at all these things very well.
I mean you see I have a problem that we are always too busy chasing the next dream.
If you don't believe me, I'll explain.
For example, the boy next door to me has taken science. As a result, people around me always date her. But I want to do Honors in Arts with English. Because I like to study English. But you may not believe that I will also start studying science. Why do you say because people will praise me? Or he has taken science means the assurance is better.
This is where we go wrong. That's why we are never good. And we follow the next dream without even knowing it.
Now you understand, how we always have to follow the

next dream.

I studied in missions since childhood so I noticed one thing. Nana didn't notice it when she was young. It's something I've thought about when I've grown up.

Several of my friends had dreams of becoming doctors, engineers, barristers, astronauts, etc. when they were below fifth grade.

Then when they were studying in class XI and XII, their dreams were so strong.

What will you do in life? Someone said I will be the greatest person in this world.

Who would say the world's most famous astronaut?

Who said I will be a cricketer?

I told them it was not possible. If someone in the world had done that, they would have told me the example of that person.

"If that person in the world can do it, why can't I?"

I was quite surprised by their confidence.

But when I told those friends about college life, what will you do in life?

It's sad to hear but it's true

That they told me would be a normal job.

You can definitely relate.

This is how our dreams slowly begin to end along with life.

And we start blaming God or circumstances.

Isn't that so?

To be honest, neither God nor circumstances are to blame for our broken dreams.

If anyone is really to blame it is our own.

Because we dream right from a young age and when it's time to make this dream come true. When we are of full working age.

or studying in college. Then we just waste time by chatting

with friends and going around. As a result we don't realize how beautifully we waste our lives.

Blame timing blames circumstances.

I mean it's not too late now.

Start today or start now.

Do what you want to do.

Do it so beautifully. And do it so much that no one else can do it better than you.

It means if you do cobbler work along railway line then do it so well and with so much love that no one else can do cobbler job better in that area.

Believe that you will earn twice the amount of money you need to survive.

We never actually do anything with our mind. When I do it, I don't give importance to that task as the next task.

So if someone ever asks you what are you doing in life?

Then you never have to say it.

I don't do anything like that.

Instead, say yes, I'm doing it.

And say it with pride.

Never look down on what you do. Think about yourself if you underestimate your work. So how do you expect others to respect your work?

The jobs I mentioned here are applicable if you are a student or if you work in an office.

Without taking a hard look at the happenings around you.

Try to look simple.

You will see that everything will be clear.

Try to understand yourself the most. Give yourself time.

Talk to yourself.

Keep calm and try to solve every problem.

One of our biggest problems is that we always want to do everything together.

Do you ever think about whether it is possible to go to Kolkata and Delhi together?
So do the work that you need to do first or the work that is most important in your life first. Do that well then what to do with the rest.
Like go where you need to go first and then go to the next one.
Hope things are clear to you.

EIGHT

WANT TO LOVE SOMEONE

The biggest problem in the world today is love.

Love is something that everyone in the world is connected with. Which is something that the whole world cannot think or imagine.

So many fairy tales, so many stories have been written about love that a person like me would find it trivial to write there.

The most valuable factor behind our well-being is love. Be it parents, be it brothers or sisters be it friends. So if we understand this thing correctly. Then I think we will get our problem solved.

Yes, of course, the great people of the world did not understand about love, so how can I understand?

But if I can explain to you what I have understood with my knowledge, then you will find the true purpose of love at least a little.

We can find very few people who have not fallen in love without knowing it. If we cry the most in life, we cry for love and if we get the most joy in life, we get it for love.

In today's era thousands of students are ruining their life by wrong path for not understanding love properly. We are among them.

I am starting very young and with simple language.

God says that He sent love to earth to experience what Jannat or Heaven would be like, which is only one percent of the happiness of Jannat.

Then you tell me that if God sends love to feel what heaven can be like, how can we suffer from it?

It will give us so much joy that we realize that if we do good deeds on earth we will go to heaven or heaven and how much happiness there will be.

But with the way love hurts us in today's society, I don't think anyone would ever want to go to heaven.

I mean, I don't think God ever lies.

Isn't that so?

Of course it is.

We start with the biggest mistake. Whenever we see a beautiful girl on the road, in any event, in school or college, we fall in love with her instantly. Since then I am busy to impress him. If I can impress him then it is done. For the first few days in the world, it seems like I am in a dream world. Then slowly when they see each other's true form, then one of them suffers and the other starts to suffer.

Isn't that so?

The first thing we need to know is what love really is?

Why do we love?

You see we have a nature if someone asks us why we love then we answer that. We need someone who will understand us and love us as we are. Share each other's words and share each other's pain. You are right.

Now I say that in my opinion it is love

"Just a name for enjoying each other's body"

If it wasn't then why love is needed. You could have developed a friendship relationship with him in general. Better than that, he could have made her a sister. These two could not even share what they could share after love, I would say they could only share their physical needs but everything else.

When our intentions are not right. So how can we be happy or good for that wrong purpose.

I am not opposing love here. I am just trying to explain the real meaning of love. If we really love someone then why do we need to touch them. Don't be patient for that. He touched her if not after marriage. And if you can't bear this much patience then how can you share the sufferings of that person at the time of danger.

Then there will be patience.

I tell you in very simple language that is why we love? There comes a time in life when we leave childhood and become adults. That's when we slowly start to get separated from our family members without even realizing it. In the same way, they start to push us away in the busyness of work. That's when we look for our failure stories or someone to make us feel a little special and that's the person we love.

You can love someone with good intentions. I don't think there is anything wrong with that. But just the same if you don't touch him. But you can swear not to trouble.

But what do we do? Make each other's parents villains. And I think the world does not understand our love. How will the world understand? Your love You yourselves do not understand what your love is.

I mean both boys and girls. Who did not understand the love of his family for so long. With your few minutes of love, he can forget the love of his family for so long. So how are

you sure. That he will not forget your love one day.
Now open your head.
Love can never hurt anyone. If that is the right way. But you see, we continue to trouble the parents, family and society with the love of the present.
If your love is so pure and if your parents can understand it. So why not marry you?
Because you want to be the best you can be. Your parents want you better than that.
Surely they think your love is not right. Because they have seen more of the world than you. That is, I am not saying that they know everything. I mean, explain to them why you would be nice to them.
The movies of our present age, who is love, present you in such a way that it seems that parents are the villains and you are the heroes.
No, parents are villains. No, you are heroes. Some are wrong with you, some are wrong with your parents.
Try to understand each other's situation and then you can find a good and correct solution. Not before that.
We used to buy clothes from small stores. Buy food from a good store. But when we choose the most precious people in our lives, we don't see anything. A quality we liked for a while. That is a reason enough for us to love someone.
And in that you feel that you will be well cared for by that person. Or you'll be fine by him. Of course you will get more trouble from him. He may leave you in future. My point is that you are the most valuable thing in your life. You will give the most precious place in your life to anyone.
Now at least think a little.
Where I am telling you to be so scrutinizing in choosing friends, I will not tell you again here.
What did you really think?

I tell you to love. Love too much, love too much.
Yes, love the girl.
But you know if you love properly.
Then you will never have to throw mud at each other during a breakup like lovers in today's society.
Build the relationships I mean. So that the person you love on the first day, just as much as you like it, just more than that, when you leave him, he will leave you on the bus. Then there should be more respect for each other. Now you might be thinking that maybe I am telling you a fairy tale.
no no no
If you start loving a girl properly, then your relationship will be better than a fairy tale.
Just think how beautiful it is to hear or tell the fairy tales we make up. Then how beautiful the stories of God made about us will be.

You may think bad, actually we do not know how to love?
Ok, I have a question that you can answer. Give the answer with your hand on your chest.
You follow three things with the one you love First Chastity I mean chastity here not just physical relationship or emotional relationship.
I mean no matter what, never touch each other before marriage or never touch each other.
Second: respect for each other. No matter how bad things got, we never lost respect for each other.
Third: Trust in each other. No matter how bad people say each other's names to you. You didn't believe it happened.
And if you can accept these three things, then you will not understand where your relationship will go.
Now you understand why I am saying your love is wrong.
Now there are many of you and we will marry each other.

So what's the point of having physical relations?
Imagine that the girl is not married to you.
Then!
Both of you cheated on those who married you later.
Isn't that so?
And you talk about love.
Hey now a days if we love someone we ask for his picture on whatsapp on the second day. If not we threaten to leave. We are going through this dirty kind of relationship. And you think this relationship will make you happy. No bad thing is good for long.
One thing to remember is that worse is worse. But if you had a holy relationship with someone then
There was no reason to leave each other.
Your family would have no reason not to accept.
And if he still leaves, then you've fallen in love with the wrong person. Or God has placed for you the girl you deserve.
Now you will say that these words are very good as a motto. Then you are totally wrong. We often don't get many things. Then we feel very bad and we resent God. To not give that thing away from us. Later, when God gives us something better than that, we understand the reason for taking that thing away from us. We can never be smarter than God. There are many times when you want nude photos of your loved ones. And if he doesn't give it to you, you might feel bad.
You would think that you couldn't do this little bit of faith.
If you think about it, you do not love his body?
Of course it is true
Will be very eager to touch loved ones. You must be patient for that. Now you might say I can't be patient.
That means it's pretty much like that, isn't it? You started

insisting that I should be a big police officer today. Is that possible? No, it is only possible if you put in enough hard work and patience and bide your time to become a cop.

Then it's time when you can be patient and wait.

So why can't you be patient for the most valuable thing in your life?

Things are so small but so profound.

When we are in any relationship with each other. Then we should try to take enough care of each other.

I mean if I make it more clear I mean that.

When your opposite partner wants to have sex with you or demands something from you for that matter.

Then you will block him mentally instead of blocking him directly. And if you don't tell him at that time, instead of understanding you, he will misunderstand you a little more.

So if you see something wrong with your partner, instead of leaving him, try to solve it from his side.

And if you think like this I will find a perfect man. Believe me you will never get it.

We will find someone perfect, better yet we will make someone perfect.

Maybe it will take some time. But the result you will get will give you a little more pleasure.

NINE

"WHAT WILL PEOPLE SAY"

The biggest one is "What will people say"?
What people will say is nothing less than a fear to us.
If you don't get a job, it's as much a problem as the people in your house. More than that, people in the neighborhood care more.
Hey, you start doing something. Why can't you do the work from all around? People will come to you with that reason.
So it is one of the biggest problems in our life.
Isn't that so?
Your daughter has run away with some boy. A few months later when you find out that they are fine. And what better news can you have than that your daughter is fine. You will immediately think of calling them home. And just then what people will say will come into your head. Then you can't bring the girl home anymore.
Suppose you fail a class. And after failing you realize your mistakes and you decide to retake the class a second time. And this time I will correct the mistakes and get good results. This will tell your mind but when you think a little

in your head you will think that if I read the same class for the second time then what will people say.
You think you want to color your hair to fulfill your hobby, you can't, you think if people say something.
Now you understand how big a problem it is. If you can't overcome it, you can never live well.
We need to understand what we need and what we don't need. Do what you think is necessary now.
One thing to remember is that you don't do anything that hurts or hurts anyone. You can do whatever you want without hurting or hurting anyone. Thousands of people say that.
People used to say that when you were young. And people still say and will continue to say in the future. So never sing to them. Because every time you listen to them, you will hurt yourself. or begging yourself to hurt them.
Remember you only get one life so don't let it go away.
You come to earth, stay for a while and then leave.
You don't want to do anything for yourself, for your family, for this world. Then God created you in vain.
I think God sends some qualities in every human being in the world. And if you don't show that value to the world. Then God gave us a gift that we missed or lost, didn't we?
Talking about people You know when people talk about you when they tried to do the same thing you are doing but they couldn't so they told you that you can't either.
Here he is not rejecting you but trying to convince you how much more worthy you are than him.
Never take what people say the wrong way.
Remember that their words will help you reach your goals. They are giving you motivation. Maybe their words are bad but their intentions are not bad.
And if you are afraid of what people say. Then not only the

work that you are doing but also you cannot do any work in front because of the fear of people.

As people say to you, why don't you get a job?

You took their words very seriously and got a government job. You think they will compliment you but you know what they will say!

"Your job is bad, the pay is low, my brother's son is your age, he earns twice as much as you."

So never try to impress them by listening to them. Because they will never be happy with anything you do.

So quit impressing them. Instead, impress those who care and love you. They will suffer if something happens to you.

Listen to them.

You will see that you have many such friends in your life. Those who make you feel better.

I mean suppose you did something. Here I try to explain with example.

Suppose you buy a car. Then your friend comes to you saying that the car is good but Rahul was saying that the color of the car is not good. I told him that this color is the best. Here they were the real motive he wanted to be nice to you. But did not understand that he hurt you. These types of people are the most terrifying. Try to stay away from them as much as you can. These are the people who you've done everything for and still say you did nothing for them. Now you understand which of your friends I am

talking

Just what you are thinking about friends.

Actually there is one thing that we can never be hurt by outsiders. Always those people who are closest to us give.

And this is what we need to understand.

People don't really go outside. People are always our relatives and friends.

Who are they actually? Creates a fear in your mind. Never consider them a part of your life.

60 to 70 thousand bad thoughts come into our head every day. And the thought that worries us the most is "What will people say?"

And the more we do this thought, the more we hand the remote control over to others.

The more we think about this the more we start listening to people. We all know these words, but why do these words remain in our heads?

Is the answer too simple?

Because they always try to hit our weak point. Because of which we are everything

Forced to listen to people despite knowing. So why do we listen to them?

If I try to analyze it a little, I will see that we are always interdependent.

I am trying to explain why I am saying this.

Suppose you go to tuition every day. So one day you thought that today you will not go to tuition, instead you will go to see a movie. On the way to the cinema, a person you know whom you call uncle. saw you Here you will fear that he will scold you if he tells you at home. Here you are not afraid of that old man. You are afraid of your parents. That's right, we're not afraid of people. I am afraid that those people should stand up, that none of us should suffer.

If I mastani on the streets. So what will people say? I think about it. The idea in it is that when the man tells my own people that I am Mastani, they will suffer for this use of me. If we try to explain it more precisely, it would be something like,

Suppose you have failed in some work in your life. You will be afraid to do the same thing the second time. If you fail this time, what will people say about you? It is a fear projected onto us. But the real fear lies within. That when we failed the first time, the people who were with us and our family members were hurt and they were hurt by me. And I don't want to fail a second time and hurt them in the same way. So I am afraid of people's words.

And that's what we have to do to get out of here. That we should think like this instead of thinking like that. We want to do that work for the second time so that the people living with us can live with their heads held high.

So when we find the right purpose of something. We don't think about people anymore.

In the way of life, always try to keep the purpose behind doing something right. You will see that you don't care what people say. Bro if we can do it. We will be able to solve this big problem.

TEN
I DON'T CARE

He was annoyed to hear the words. Hey, you'll find content ranging from social media to television. I don't care about anyone.

Class five students write in their bio. I don't care what they say to the world. And now there's one more thing. Now we show the middle finger to show that I don't care. To show yourself cool in the eyes of society.

When I was studying in class twelve. Then I used to see that on the day when Mother's Day was read, everyone wrote Happy Mother's Day as a status. He used to give pictures of his mother.

But I could not give. That's why I'm a bit shy. I also thought that I love my mother so much, so why am I not giving it to her? Again, I used to see everyone giving status when someone in their family died. But I could not give. I felt very guilty then. But slowly when I learned to understand, I saw that when something cares for us or someone cares for us, we do not understand their importance. When someone left we realized the status. I never gave a status because my love never waned. When your man dies. Then you can't put his status.

So we say we don't care.

I don't say it because I don't care, I say it because I care. Because if you don't care about something, you won't think about it. So why do you write that I don't care?

First of all, we care about everything. When we don't like a person, we don't tell everyone that we don't like him, but we don't go to places where people talk about him.

not so

Second, why do you think that caring is bad?

Must understand, must know.

I don't understand how many times I have made others suffer to show myself cool in front of everyone.

We must care We must care. If we take care of someone, he will take care of us.

Think once, why should I mistreat someone who is treating me well? Will it ever be okay to show that?

Why show the middle finger?

when you grow up Then you know when you open your Facebook and see that you have uploaded a picture by showing the middle finger. You know that day you will laugh at yourself and think how stupid you were.

Do you want your children to look at those pictures and imagine what their parents were like?

Remember one thing, what we are doing now depends on how our future will be. If we don't do a single mistake now, we must pay for it in the future.

We always expect good behavior from the frontman if we have a problem. But we do not treat anyone well. Now maybe you will say

you are wrong Yes we behave well when you say so when we have an interest. The people of the world are not selfish, we are selfish. We will say that we do not care about anyone and that people will care about us.

It would be wrong if I used the word I don't care. Now they say why do we care?

If you think about it, you will see that when we were children, we didn't care about anyone.

It means if you are placed in the arms of an IPS officer as a child. And if you feel like it at that time, you will do it immediately.

You don't for once wonder whose lap you're in.

That's right.

But if I ask you to stand in front of an IPS officer, you will be afraid to stand.

Right!

Tell me how it was created. It is created out of fear. Because if you see when you were young you didn't listen to anyone. Besides, you didn't care about anyone. But slowly as you grow older, everyone from your relatives to the soc starts to respect you. Begins to ban smashing.

As you think, don't do this, don't do that, if you do this, you will be harmed. You will get sick if you do that. We get used to hearing such words from childhood. As a result when we reach adulthood.

Then we don't have that child anymore. We keep getting rejection by so many times in life. Which slowly makes us afraid to even think about small things. I can do it.

This society kills the brave in us. As a result, we grow,w but we become scared.

As a result, whatever we do, we start feeling afraid to do everything. Better yet, we see the downsides of starting a job. And stop there. It is our biggest disease.

If you look at it, you'll see I said early in the book how people become afraid of dreaming as they grow up. I mean any kid who if you ask what do you want to be? You will see he will say Doctor Engineer Astronaut etc. But if you ask him after 22 years what you want to be. Then the boy will say that even a small job will do. It is a fear created by our failure. Slowly our good nature is disappearing where is the brave truth.

Have? y ou ever thought about this before?

I hope not.

It's not a question of not caring.

We have to go inside the problems and understand them. Otherwise, we will never be able to find solutions to the problems above.

I mean we have to awaken the dying being in our mind or the brave being. Until we can awaken it, we cannot be well. No matter how much we grow up, we should never kill the child in us.

Now talking about how the brave child in us died?

You may think the answer is difficult but not at all.

In factWeilled this entity through our many small mistakes. As you think we have never studied by heart. As a result we did, not perform well in class. Then you will see that we will be afraid to read. Whenever we are afraid of something. Just as slowly the brave within us will die.

But here the soc did not kill the brave truth. I died because of your own mistakes.

so

I have been saying from the beginning of the book that we have to see everything very precisely in order. Know which one we need.

No more.

How to tell now is also very simple. Correct your mistakes that can still be corrected. And keep it in your head so that you don't make unnecessary mistakes. If you If yourself on the simple and true path, then that brave truth will never die in you.

As long as the illusion of the world increases in our mind, wrong actimindsand wrong paths will continue through us. As long as these continue, the brave child within us will continue to die.

As a result, we will continue to fail in everything we do. Every time we fail, frustration, sadness, jealousy, anger, etc. will descend on us.

It is really difficult to say something verbally and convert it into reality. We need to understand how exactly what we are saying corresponds to reality. Because we are creating a wrong image in the eyes of people in society through the wrong message which is not necessary at all.

Now you may have a question in your mind again, you said a little earlier that you don't obey the society. Aglow you say society has to obey. First of all I never said that in society is not to be obeyed. Because believe it or not we complement each other. So you are without society and society can never develop without you. Simply put, we can never do without each other. Think about what you are talking about. You will live in that society and I will not call you a member of society. Or you will neglect the society in which you live.

Society can never be bad. You have to remember that everything has everything one is bad and the other is good. And this is no exception.

My intention could never be to ask you to be alone. Because you won't be good alone.

By now I hope you understand who we should say we don't care about and who we shouldn't. If you ask me, I'd say no one should be told. Why do you say so, someone, you don't like?

ELEVEN

PARENTS, DON'T UNDERSTAND ME

If there is anyone closest to us in the world, it is these two fathers and mothers. But whenever we are a little older. When we grow up not mentally but physically. Then we don't like parents. In the modern era, we constantly prove our parents wrong to make ourselves look smart. We forget that it is by holding their hands that we begin to speak.

Nowadays we all have a complaint. You will see that I want to do that, but my father does not allow me to do that. Or I want to buy it, but the mother doesn't buy it.

Nowadays we have influenced ourselves so much in social media that. We think the direction they have given us is correct. It means they will see one thing and follow your passion. And since then we started following. Then we started making demands

I want to be a singer so I will leave my studies.

I want to paint.

I want to act

I started talking to my parents. And then we are scolded by them and we think that they are not with us. They don't understand me. Since then we start doing whatever we like. Out of pride, we start to stop talking to our parents. Not talking to our parents. As a result, we never realize when we are slowly drifting away from them. Without them, we have started organizing our lives. I started walking alone. Now tell us who is to blame here or our parents? Nor did they ever ask us to separate from them. To put it more simply, you have never told them what you want to be. So how do they know what you want to be? If you can't find your talent in any subject, how can they find it in you?

Think once you have a son who came to you and said father I will not study. I will be a cricketer. How would you like it? No, he has played any big matches before. Maybe he didn't play with anyone except the neighborhood boys. He doesn't even play better than all the boys in the neighborhood. He insists to you that he will become a cricketer just by hitting a few sixes one day and encouraging the village people.

Now he says you will accept him by giving up his studies.

never

Remember one thing. Every decision we make is connected to the past. Maybe your parents wanted to do something in life but they didn't get to do it. Due to various difficulties, they may be seeing their past in your decision.

A past where there is only destruction.

So think about it, they don't want you to be spoiled like them. So don't get angry with them about things. Explain things to them. Let them see what you are trying to do. You are doing it right. You will find that your parents will buy all the things you need to do your job no matter how expensive it is.

Once you understand them, you will get all the answers.

You know, there are some things in life that we don't understand until we go there. So is the place of parents.

No matter how much I mean to you. No matter how many thousands of novels you read, you won't understand them until you become someone's father. When you see everything will seem clear to you. Today you will have clear answers to the questions you want to ask your parents.

But then you go back and feel guilty for doing bad things to them.

You will find it hard to spend time with them.

You will want to hug them and cry. But maybe you will see that they are not in this world.

And then you will be looking for your father among the older people. Talk to them now instead of finding your father later. You laugh heartily with them.

Smile. You may not know how much you mean to them. You know that no matter how much they are in trouble if you speak in front of them once with a smile, all their sorrows and troubles will disappear.

Now notice one thing you will see that now we go from village to city to study or work. We don't want to introduce our parents in our village to prove ourselves always superior there.

I think, my parents don't wear that kind of clothes, what will my friends say?

What if my girlfriend thinks I'm poor and leaves?

Remember one thing, those who truly love you don't care what you look like. Where did you come from? So every person you are with is involved in your life. So never separate them. It is a matter of pride for you that you have parents, whatever they are, they are your parents. So never hide them.

They are your pride.

TWELVE

OVERTHINKING

It's almost 2:30 PM now.

The revision of this book is almost complete. Just then I suddenly remembered this chapter. This chapter is so important whenever I think that if this chapter is not written in the book then the original purpose of this book will be completely defeated.

So I stopped editing the book for a while and started writing this chapter.

"extra thought"

You may wonder if thinking is such a bad thing.

Overthinking is such a big disease that you can't even imagine how exactly it can harm you.

The biggest thing is that patients with this disease do not realize that they have such a disease.

You may not believe that more than 80 percent of people in the world suffer from overthinking.

Let me first give you some examples of how this thinking kills you, so it will be helpful to discuss this.

For example, I don't know how to ride a bike till today. You know why I feel like I might have a major accident if I learn to drive it. I think those who don't know how to ride a bike yet. The only reason they don't know is that they think they might have a major accident.

But on the other hand, almost everyone knows how to ride a bike. So riding a bike is not very difficult. But because of your thoughts, I or people like me can never ride a bike.

Let me give you another example of the school you attend or the company you work for.

Suppose the owner of that company called you suddenly and said that today is Saturday and when you come on Monday, there is a very important thing to do with you. Or if you are studying in school then your teacher said to you that you have a meeting on Monday, see you at the office.

Believe it or not, you will be thinking from that day until Monday why did you call me sir?

Or why my office boss called me?

You will often feel like you have been called out for doing something wrong. When you went means when that desired Monday came and you went and saw that the teacher called you, for this reason, there is a function in your school ahead, so you will be given several responsibilities.

And your boss called you because it's Monday to take your boss's car to take his wife to the market.

But 99% of the thoughts that will come to your mind during those two days will be bad thoughts.

And your brain will make the situation worse by thinking.

That means your brain will try to think worse than the maximum it can think.

I hope this is easy for you to understand by now.

Think of yourself as a victim of such diseases.

Worrying is not a bad thing, but excessive thinking is enough to drive you crazy.

But if we stop thinking then we will never be able to do

anything or make any progress in our life.

We need to recognize when our thoughts are turning negative.

Think we can't stop anyone. Because we are called thinking beings because we think. But in this chapter, I will show you some simple methods by which you can understand when you are thinking bad and when you are thinking good.

As a result, whenever you think badly, your brain will give you a signal that you have started thinking badly. And it will be possible to do this only when you read this chapter completely.

We must first understand where such bad thoughts originate from.

or where the origin is.

There is so much misinformation and bad information constantly entering our brains around us that it causes a kind of layering in our brains. And that lining is bad.

As I make it a little easier for you.

You start watching news channels for a week in a row.

You will see that only thoughts will come into your head about how bad the world is and how bad the people around you are. You will even start thinking about your parents and whether they are treating you right.

But at that point, if you stop watching news channels for seven days. Then you will see how beautiful this world is and how good the people around you are.

This is because of wrong information entering our brains.

The same goes if you fall in love with the wrong person. And if that person continues to harm you, then your faith in people will be lost.

On the other hand, if you meet a good person, you will feel that the whole world is full of good people.

So when we enter any book, any person, any place, any kind

of information into our brain. Before that, we need to check whether what I am taking is exactly what I need or is good for me. Then you don't have to overthink in many parts or you can control yourself completely before you get to the point of overthinking.

Second, we never think about the present. Most of the time we think about the future if not the past. And this is one of the reasons why we overthink.

Because we read guest most of the time in our life. In retrospect, we think about our mistakes. And thinking that if we could go back in time we would have corrected this mistake. As we always do when we are young we think we will grow up and when we are older we think that being young was good.

Think about it from both sides, neither of these two is possible.

But it would have been more beneficial for us if we had enjoyed that childhood when we were young in that place. Similarly, if we enjoy the benefits that we get when we are older.

Then it is more beneficial for us.

Thirdly:

You might not believe it. The more empty we are. The less we do, the more thoughts come into our heads.

If you think about it, you will see that on the days when you are so busy with work, you don't have a chance to do anything else, let alone think about it.

Let me tell you something funny.

For those who masturbate, quitting is a very difficult task. But if they stay in the hospital for a month. Then you will see that they will not remember for once. There is no such thing as masturbation.

So we should try to be busy as much as possible. Because

we don't work in the present it makes us think that the past was better for us. Because if your present is good then you will never think about your past. or about the future.
We simply need to understand that no matter how hard we try, there are some things we can never change.
And it would be completely foolish for us to change them.
One of the reasons for overthinking is that we are always comparing.
Sometimes with myself.
Sometimes with own family members with other family members.
And whenever we do, we don't get the results we expect. And that's when we overthink. Like you see someone else's wife and you like her. Then you start comparing with your wife.
You know what is the most problematic thing you try to match the bad things of your wife with the good things of your other wife.
But you don't understand that you are seeing only the good qualities of the above wife. Maybe if you were to see the bad qualities of the other's wife then maybe you wouldn't even approach her.
So we need to stop comparing.
I will end this chapter with one last point without making this chapter too big. If we enlarge any chapter. Then it will be a little difficult to understand. My aim is always to make my words understandable to the readers.

THIRTEEN

FAKE WORLD

Fake fake fake......

The word fake is very familiar and used these days. Today, everything you look at, buy, eat, and read has this word fake.

Along with the things slowly people don't know why it seems fake. Even their usage seems fake, isn't it?

This word is like poison to us nowadays. spread around. This needs to be stopped now.

Because this is the thing that prevents us the most from good. So we must find out where this word is used in our life.

We have to stop those things. Until we can stop that, we will not be good.

Now trying to analyze things slowly.

Today we love to show people. If you don't believe it, just look at any person's social media such as WhatsApp, Facebook, and Instagram. And go there and see their lifestyle. It would seem that one Dhoni is better than the other. It seems that there is no problem in their life. And if you see them in real life, you will see that one is suffering more than the other. One is poorer than the other. We are busy trying to prove that we are bigger than them.

No matter how many problems we have in our life.

We have slowly forgotten what we need. What do we need?

I just have to take it now that we've got it.

How long will we continue to fulfill the next dreams?

Don't stay and he took it, I don't need it, so why should I take it?

I am starting with a small story, I used to study in a hostel in Burdwan. Everyone was smoking cigarettes there. So one day I sat next to a boy eating and asked him, brother, why are you smoking cigarettes?

I eat like this to show myself modern.

Hey, eat too, it's a trend these days. All men do not play it again. And besides, it cannot be enjoyed without playing.

If you want to be modern, do you have to smoke cigarettes? Not at all.

You are smoking to make yourself better than others or like others.

You don't need it and you don't need it to be a model.

You are studying in college now so it seems that you will understand when you are older and when you can't leave it for a few days. It was never a trend.

And then you see it and you can't leave it, it's too late.

As a result, I have never smoked a cigarette till today, because I felt that I did not have good quality myself.

That means I'm not belittling people who eat.

This is exactly how we are always misrepresenting ourselves.

We all consider ourselves celebrities these days. Trying to show their life in front of people. And it starts right from here that boy bought a good camera and I need it too. You may not understand. That we were never celebrities. Now we are young so getting time to show ourselves celebrities.

When you don't get You to know how bad you'll feel when you face reality. Who were you showing? And the most important thing is that while presenting this false life in front of everyone, you have stopped enjoying your life.

First of all, where is your life? But you know why you are not happy. Because you are trying to follow someone else's life instead of enjoying your own life.

Hey, nowadays we all want to be social influencers means YouTubers.

Really?

And for this to happen, good boys are doing this by leaving their studies. Why do you feel that education is preventing you from achieving your dreams? The problem is not here. Ever since smartphones became available in our hands. Since then we have started to adopt vain people as our ideals. And what they are saying now is like a line of symptoms to us. Hey, the one you think is your ideal, first see what he does. Does he deserve to be your ideal? Education never hinders your dreams but helps to transform your dreams into reality.

And besides, not every one of us is made to do everything. When I see someone I follow them and think this is for me. That's when we begin to drift away from success in our lives. Hey, I used to think like them that everything is for every man. And thinking of this I started learning music. And started learning guitar believe me again there was no lack of effort. But I will never be a singer. My voice is not good. I wasn't cut out for it. Then I thought I would be a motivational speaker. Because I was made for it.

So learn to understand things. Never make anyone your ideal. If you want to discuss it, then a whole book can be written.

Not without saying one thing.

Today we are so involved in the false world that we are afraid to expose ourselves to everyone
Can't believe it.
Today we are always preferring the false world by withdrawing from real life. Today we are covering our true beauty with a filter. Today we are exposing our bodies in front of everyone to get some likes and comments.
Do we always say that girls wear extra-quality makeup?
Have you ever wondered why they put on extra makeup?
for you
Because we have never loved any black or dark-skinned girl. When we gave them a place in our dreams. I didn't give them because we are just fairy tale books
Want to be bound by it. Believe that you are better than the girl in the filter. original
Love the girl outside the filter. That day the girl will stop giving filters.
You will be surprised that the world is connected with the life of each of us. One of our decisions has the power to change the world.
So if we can recognize the real thing
People will start giving us authentic stuff even if they charge a bit more.
It depends on us what we do.
Because when we begin to enter the real world from the false world. We will no longer be afraid of showing anyone to lose.
And we will start living well.
This false world has begun. By some false people. And by this we misunderstand.
It can be changed only then. When we start getting educated. The importance of education in our society will continue to grow. I am not asking you to change the

importance of education.

I say educate yourself. Educate yourself if you can. By educated here I am talking about educated in the real sense. Then you will not step into the false world with your knowledge.

You can then bring out those who choose to live in a false world.

This is how we should start it.

FOURTEEN

CREATE YOUR OWN WORLD

We came to the last chapter to watch. I did not think that I would write so many pages. I don't know why I developed a relationship with you so I don't want to end it. Tears of farewell came with a strange joy. I have never told anyone so openly. You will remember this book every time you read it. I am an ordinary boy than you. Who dreams of changing himself like you. He wants to introduce himself to the society. And I want to create a meaning in the true meaning of my life. Like you, I want to do good for people around me. By writing this book I do not want to introduce myself to you as a writer. I want to say that I am a version of you. I just want to remind you of the words. I am your friend who wants to help you achieve your dreams. The words I will say now are the most valuable words in this book.

You may think that the name of this chapter is why I spelled my own world?

Till now I talked about presenting myself in front of this world. Let's create a world of our own. Where there will be only those we love and those who love us. Each thing will be like itself. Just like a fantasy.

Then what you need to be prepared for is to face some harsh realities of this world.

can you There will be some failures.

Let's go then

The sooner you go through life the sooner you can accept this fact.

How was your day today?

are you ok

The number of people asking these questions will gradually decrease as you get older. In fact, what happened to you does not matter to anyone in the world. So you have to accept the hard truth first. You have to teach yourself something new every day. It means you have to remember every day that you learn something new every day. Because if you don't learn by yourself. So why would people want to live in your world? You have to change yourself first. Maybe it will take time, it will take a lot of time, but you have to be patient and change yourself. Change yourself.

The second hard truth we have to accept is that everyone we love with our hearts will one day leave us. So we must always be ready. I will never tell you to surrender yourself to others. I would say love every person as much as you deserve without demeaning yourself. just as much Then you will see that you will never suffer.

You will make friends by following the rules that I told you about choosing friends. They may not stay with you for life. So you have to prepare yourself again. First make some rules for your life. Means exactly how many people you want to take around you. I mean think if you decide that you will only have 10 friends in your life. So if someone leaves you. Wait for him for a while. After that time has passed another new friend from the rule of picking friends at that place

Put it in its place. It is true that this is sad to hear. If you can't do this you will never be good in life. So you have to do it.

Don't get into small matters unnecessarily. It means if there is a fight going on in the street, see if it is possible for you to stop it from a distance. If not then no need to go there. Instead, call those who can prevent it. Because you have to keep in mind that you are not a superhero. And if you keep looking at such small incidents, you will keep getting hurt again and again.

You have to toughen yourself up a bit.

You need to know how important social media is to you. Discontinue use if not needed. Because it's behind you not being happy

Has the most roles. Like if you watch a motivational video at night and think you will start everything in life from tomorrow. Let's say you're a bit fat and you decide to start running tomorrow. How good is your decision. But tomorrow when you wake up in the morning you will find that a friend who is fatter than you has built a six pack body. The motivational video you watched yesterday will immediately seem trivial to you and you will begin to suffer from depression. You will not for once see that he created his six pack body using filters. But if you had not opened the Facebook app at that place, you would have finished your first run by now. So uninstall the apps if you don't need them. The job you are doing now or if you are in school or college, where you are or where you are working. Wrong there

Stop making mistakes. And start using the good points there. And think what you can do with them. He has your benefit. There is no point in catching mistakes here and there. Everyone is a motivational speaker on social media these days. So stop mistaking them. Give him a word or two if you like him or feel you need them in your life. Then forget about them. You may feel like you have time now. In fact, the least thing we have is time. So start valuing time. If you're playing games, you're doing it wrong. Do things to reach your goal in that place. It benefits you. Don't listen to people at all. You are completely different from everyone else. So do the work you do with so much love. As if this work is more than you

No one can do a good job. No one has ever done it before. It is very important to work every day. Because if you don't work, you will never be able to create a beautiful world for yourself.

Nowadays there is a saying, you will see we want freedom. But remember too much freedom always makes us reckless. So bind yourself within the rules. It will help you reach your goals. Stop hanging out with friends too much. Read some good books instead. Take a walk when you have time. You will get a chance to know yourself a little while working. You will realize how much worse people are than you. How much do you need in the world. And then you will feel bad to waste your life in vain. I always think we should travel outside so we can realize how insignificant we are compared to this world.

As a result, if there is any pride in our mind, it will be destroyed.

Make yourself as if everyone you're with misses you the most when you leave them. They say I had a friend. really good

But your life is worth it. Only then will you find your true self. Never change yourself.

Isn't it surprising? Throughout the book I told you to

change and in the last chapter I told you not to change.

I am not asking you to change like that. You will see that when we dream to do something in life, our intention is never bad. Let me explain more clearly

It means if you want to be a good officer first of all when you want to be a good officer you have the intention to sit in that chair.

Can always do good to people. But when we get that chair or fulfill that dream. Then we forget our real purpose and start serving our own interests through that chair. As a result we start walking in the wrong direction. Fear of getting caught starts to creep into our minds. And then we forget to be good. But think once you complete your dream. And your intentions remained the same. Then you can create a beautiful environment. He used to get the love of a hundred people. That brave truth would have awakened in you. And you would start living well.

right?

You will see that many people will give you a lot of trouble on the way in life, many times you will get hurt. But forgive them. Because remember that many people will come into your life along the way, some of them will give you a lot of trouble. And some people will teach you to love. It will give some beautiful moments. So forget their bad sides and move forward with these moments of those who gave you good moments. You will be much better. If you can forgive them. Then you will see that one day when they realize their mistake they will love you the most. To them you will be no less than a superhero.

We are not here on earth to live forever. Then why so much anger and pride. There are so many people in the world if you start hanging out with one every day your life will pass. But there will be no people on earth. So what is the use of being angry with someone rather forget him and be a new one

Socialize with people.

Don't mix with a limited number of people all the time. If you socialize with new people sometimes, they will help you to forget your past. You can present yourself to people in a new way. It benefits you a lot.

And we can build a beautiful world through these. I need your hand to build. Let's all change the society in a beautiful way. We may not be the richest people in the world. But I can be one of the ten people around us. Because it is in our hands.

Society really needs a good person like you so don't waste yourself.

I don't want to go but I have to finish. Because everything has an end. Or better yet, whatever has a beginning has an end. So I ended here. This is my first book so I don't have that kind of experience. In the meantime, if I ever trouble you. Then forgive me. Actually I forgot to tell you my name is The MOMI no no it's to show my people. But you can call me Mominul. I didn't study literature so I don't have much linguistic knowledge. Please forgive me if there are any mistakes. And if you have any problems in your life then you can definitely message me and I will try to solve them as your personal friend. I want to give you the number. Ok you do one thing you message me @mominul_amin. I will answer.

Be well, be healthy, take care of yourself,

End Note

*We need to understand what is really needed to be well.
* Money, money, friends, these are not the criteria of being well, they can only help a little to be well.
*Choose the right friends in life.
*It is better to have no friends than bad friends.
*Try to choose a good partner instead of sacrificing everything for love.
*Keep waiting to enjoy the results of what you do, it can be a good deed or a good bad deed.

thank you